i599,322
L5764

Kangaroos

Steve Parish

ANIMALS are Fun!

For a free color catalog describing Gareth Stevens Publishing's list of high-quality books and multimedia programs, call 1-800-542-2595 (USA) or 1-800-461-9120 (Canada). Gareth Stevens Publishing's Fax: (414) 225-0377.

Library of Congress Cataloging-in-Publication Data available upon request from the publisher. Fax: (414) 225-0377 for the attention of the Publishing Records Department.

ISBN 0-8368-2614-0

First published in North America in 2000 by
Gareth Stevens Publishing
1555 North RiverCenter Drive, Suite 201
Milwaukee, WI 53212 USA

This edition © 2000 by Gareth Stevens, Inc. First published in 1998 by Steve Parish Publishing Pty Ltd, P. O. Box 1058, Archerfield, BC, Queensland 4108, Australia. Photography and creative direction by Steve Parish, with special thanks to Hans and Judy Beste (pp. 6 bottom left, 10, 11) and Ian Morris (p. 6, top left). Text by E. Melanie Lever, Kate Lovett, and Pat Slater, SPP. Additional end matter © 2000 Gareth Stevens, Inc.

U.S. author: Amy Bauman

Printed in United States of America

1 2 3 4 5 6 7 8 9 04 03 02 01 00

Gareth Stevens Publishing
MILWAUKEE

A kangaroo is a warm-blooded mammal called a marsupial.

All female marsupials have a pouch in which a baby grows.

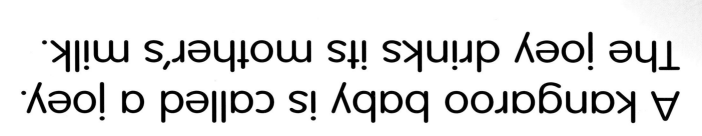

A kangaroo baby is called a joey.
The joey drinks its mother's milk.

Someday, the joey will leave its mother and travel on its own.

The kangaroo has many relatives — the wallaroo, the bettong, the

quokka, the potoroo, the tree-
kangaroo, and the rock wallaby.

A kangaroo eats grasses and leaves. It sleeps during the day.

It hops on its strong hind legs, searching for food and water.

The tree-kangaroo is a small
kangaroo that lives in trees.

Potoroos and bettongs dig in the ground for plants and insects.

Red kangaroos and eastern gray kangaroos live in groups.

These kangaroos eat from late afternoon to early morning.

If a wallaroo finds enough plants
to eat, it does not need water.

The wallaby is a small kangaroo that eats leaves and grasses.

A kangaroo...

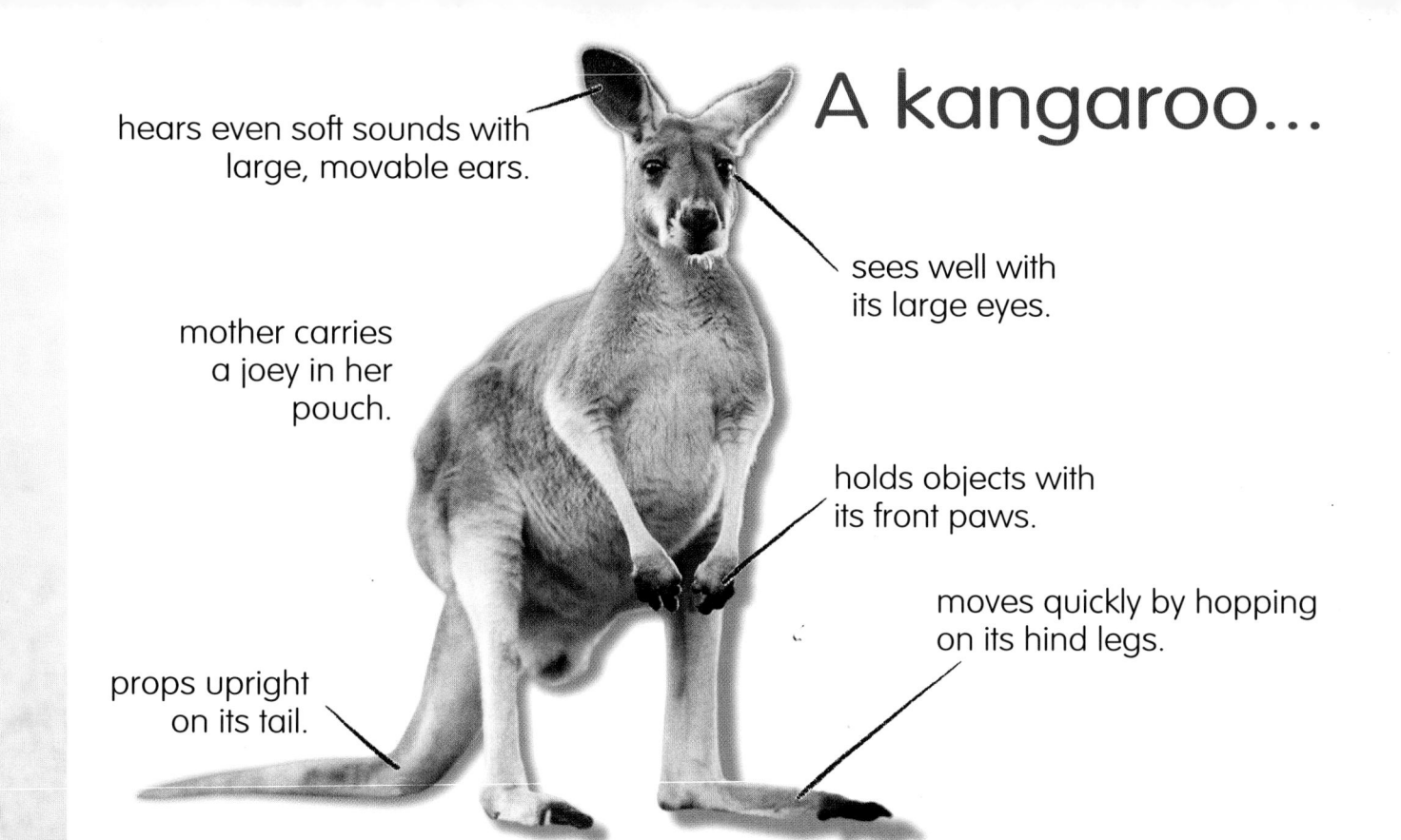

hears even soft sounds with large, movable ears.

sees well with its large eyes.

mother carries a joey in her pouch.

holds objects with its front paws.

moves quickly by hopping on its hind legs.

props upright on its tail.

Glossary/Index

hind legs — back legs 9

joey — a baby kangaroo 4, 5

mammal — any of a large group of warm-blooded animals whose young are nourished with milk from the mother's body ·2

marsupial — a mammal, such as the kangaroo, koala, and opossum, that carries its young in the mother's pouch 2, 3

pouch — a pocket-like opening on the belly, such as that of the kangaroo, for carrying babies 3

relatives — animals that are related or connected to other animals by their ancestry 6

warm-blooded — having a high and constant body temperature that operates independently of, and does not change with, the surroundings   2